Orbital Debris

Poems
By

Amy Lerman

Winner of
the Jonathan Holden
Poetry Chapbook Contest

Judged by Laura Read

Choeofpleirn Press ~ Leavenworth, Kansas
2022

ISBN: 979-8-218-03149-7

Also available from Choeofpleirn Press
Fran Schumer Weight (Finalist of JH Poetry Chapbook Contest)

Choeofpleirn Press
Leavenworth, KS 66048
choeofpleirnpress@gmail.com
www.choeofpleirnpress.com

"You're an interesting species. An interesting mix. You're capable of such beautiful dreams, and such horrible nightmares. You feel so lost, so cut off, so alone; only you're not. See, in all our searching, the only thing we've found that makes the emptiness bearable, is each other."

Carl Sagan

Table of Contents

Part I:

Ground Control

Why Is It?

Every time I go to the bank, I feel like I'm on a soap opera
set, where the silk-bloused tellers busy piles of file folders,
which, I'm sure, like on television, only hold take-out
menus. Every time I eat raw carrots, I hiccup, yet no other food
edits my breathing. Every time I see my sister, a lunch
or a quick return of my nephew's phone charger, we cheek
kiss three times, an affectation turned habit. Every time I
lose the lottery I'm surprised, though I play it three times
a year maybe. Every time I tell you Metallica's lead singer
lives down our street, you laugh, and don't get me
wrong, I'm glad you get my humor, but really he does,
wear your glasses, your not recognizing him isn't on me.
Every time I hear "Comfortably Numb," I taste opium,
my tongue circling its sweet residue on my lips, but I never
hallucinated, it couldn't have been pure, still we bragged
how the elevator's floor rippled. Every time I fuck
up the dishwasher by bending the top roller's plastic
disc, I remind you of my idiocy, apologize, lift my shirt,
my tits, thank god, still bankable. Every time I leave a room,
I announce it even though you can see me moving. Every
time I line my eyes, I'm tempted to draw tears, oversized,
infantile-looking drops along my cheekbones. Every time I
get a pedicure I am shamed for not giving birth, more than
when my grandmother questions or my students look
confused, the constant, Oh, but you'd make such a great
mother
combined, every fucking time, over fifteen years already,
just let it go, I've made my peace, why can't they? Every time,
I promise not to curse, I break the promise within minutes
because God damn it, every time I depress the garage door
opener,
I break a goddamned nail, just as every time you—
outlined by the kitchen light and door frame,
wave the car, me, in.

Mimeograph

It's weird how my fingertips purple
when I'm healthiest, thawing blueberries
meant for oatmeal, more years without
medication, and how I've always been drawn
to staining, particularly purpled fingertips,
all those carboned pads my sister and I used
when playing store or restaurant, setting up
a great aunt's hat boxes like Oleson's general store
on *Little House on the Prairie*, always delivering
my parents' receipts for invisible tuna melts.
After hours, we'd need to use the scrub brush
until purple turned fingers red, the cleaning
delayed by the ink's figure eights swirling
the basin and our need to trace them.

At a summer camp years later, I re-inked every
time I flattened master stencils—canteen or KP
schedules—against the Gestener's cylinder,
the purple's smell lavender yet medicinal
like alcohol-dipped cotton balls, lingering—
intoxicating, night after night, as I held his hand
on the cabin porch, until he needed to return
to his side of the lake and a letter from his girl.

Now, I wonder if that ink ever left, if I didn't
scrub hard enough, year after year spilling
deeper into dermal layers, a continuous threading,
paper to paper, index finger to thumb.
All I know is I am not alone, this purple
resurging in every restaurant serving squid
ink risotto, where prep cooks and sous chefs
forego gloves, polka-dot crisp, white aprons,
which memorialize the gutting, ink sac
and tentacle trimming, behind-the-eye stabbing,
making us allies, our purpling palpable, all labors
and years now obsidian, transferable, irregular, blobs.

You Always Knew

I missed the ocean,
so you drove me south, past Trimble, the town named
for your uncle, the neon flashing "Ska"
among the burned-out bulbs for "Skateland,"
to the gravel pit
where Old Highway 50 met Haven Road.
I'm not sure what I expected—

mounds of crumbling rock, beheaded beer bottles,
a grayish puddle--
but what lay ahead was a valley of blue
water so still, so sprawling, so deserted,
it looked like an aerial photo from space—
the one
you tacked to my ceiling, for somewhere to look
or float into when sleep shunned me,
became your mistress.

You grinned at my silence, stroked
my left thigh, home to your hand
for most of the trip, then pulled me
out of the pickup, single-file style,
to the water's edge. As you slid

down my cutoffs, I reached
for your shirt collar, planned to stretch
it over your head, but stopped
at the hoop in your ear,
fingered that small part of you,
until your hand cupped mine,
and as nascent, synchronized swimmers,
we drifted,
until the whole, silly blue enveloped us.

~~You, Yourself, Are Still Okay~~

If you enter that large room, you will see rows
and rows of boxes stacked like the train trestle
outside of town, and should you move toward
the corner labelled with your last name, you will
see an envelope slanted to fit the box's edges.
Don't be concerned when you see your full name
typewritten on its front or when you unseal
the triangle behind, the signature at the letter's
edge will be familiar, friendly—*Gerry*—
and you will smile anticipating encouraging
words among the many, single-spaced paragraphs.

I know your defense is in two days, you will read,
such a kind professor who insisted on an A+
semesters ago, how you bonded over Updike,
and Monday morning, he will smile and applaud
your hard work, a *pièce de résistance* you imagine
him saying, as he will rise from his chair.

But, you are not ready.

You will feel cliched, as you read this,
since your body will halt, "freeze," if you will,
two hundred and fifty pages saved in desk
and t-shirt drawers, ready to be bound, engraved—

                     Maybe, I should've said
something sooner.

Six, extraocular muscles will rotate your sockets,
side to side, then downward, words will rise
from the page, as grad school years will roll,
reverse, conflate and shock you back
to a British lit. seminar, that tragic Little Father

Time's murder-suicide note

Done because we are too menny.

and your paper on the power of epistles.
Somehow, you will finish the page, the details of his not
feeling
right, well, his daughter's new baby not even bringing him
smiles, he needs more walks, he thinks, some time away,
nevertheless, he will not sit around the table nor sign
off for you, *I'm running out of space*, he will insist—

Remember, you yourself are still okay.

But, you will not read his last words, those wood
boxes compelling you, your body forward.
You might not realize that you will refold,
reflap, even retilt the envelope
in its awkward house, then trace its cool, hard
edges until someone asks how you are,
comments on the storm last night,
the sounds of the afternoon train whistle
seeping through cracked windows,
lingering in the room.

Living Below Sea Level

You could always tell the change of season
by the Publix bag reminders to stock up
on batteries, canned foods, and candles,
plus, in Hurricane Season tradition, my parents
would retell stories of life before me, my sister,
their apartment windows the only not to blow,
their living room a refuge for neighbors. Every
year, I'd wait for a hurricane, that chance
to masking tape our windows in "Xs" under
Dad's supervision, so, as he would explain,
glass would chunk rather than shatter. I can't
recall how many times we would prepare
overnight bags, some cat toys, our four-inch,
portable television, and head north, inland,
at four stories high, my grandmother's condo
a much safer location. My sister and I would let
the cat wander her new environs, spread sleeping
bags in the dining room, then run to bedroom
windows framing nothing more than threaded
rain and slated skies, while the adults poured
Chianti and watched local updates. After hours,
we would all semi-sleep until the 5:00 AM
alarm—the one my sister and I set—would lever
us upright for the moments, according to forecasters,
of greatest impact. So often, though, no winds
ruptured palm fronds, no storm eye quieted, no school
got cancelled, in spite of our loyalty, our sacrifice,
our willingness to monitor, that taping and alarm naught,
our only celebration some early morning chocolate milk
and extra bowls of Alpha Bits.

No Shoes Required

When we shared a bedroom, my sister and I loved *The Room
Is Mine*, a story of sisters who divided their own bedroom
with a jump rope. Like those sisters, we stretched the rope
vertically, then stood on either side, our toes tickling the shag
carpet, as we repeated their dialogue, "Everything on this
side is mine," I, the proud owner of a hurricane window
and *The Wizard of Oz* poster, my sister's settlement portion,
a small desk and the room's door. During those separations,
I would pretend to have a bicycle awaiting on the roof—
Dad had shown us how to crawl out the window if ever
there was a fire—so I could still exit, my hair immediately
forming into silky braids despite Florida humidity, my feet
propelling me skyward until landing me in a technicolor
world of endless paths, only the happy parts of Dorothy's
adventure—no flying monkeys or green-faced witches—,
nor older sister telling me "I won't be your friend anymore"
if I didn't bring her cookies, or crew-cutting my Malibu
Barbie's once-waisted hair when she promised "it would be
a trim," no—

there would just be me—

singing along with these weird, new friends who didn't
care how sweat-stained my checkered dress, my bare
feet skipping as far as I could go.

Part II:

Breathing Space

Incubation

I hope you won't mind when I unzip
your body and crawl inside. I promise

to be quiet and gentle around your vena
cava, settling into your cavity like one

of the cats, so you'll barely know I'm there.
I'm not trying to crowd you or codepend:

I just can't bear the insomnia any longer, staring
at my eyelids minute after minute, all I can see

are circles, rotating halos when I try to sleep,
I just feel so dizzy and yearn for your respirations.

And, don't worry: I have washed the remnant glue
globbing my hair from the sleep study's electrodes,

and I will not overperfume, plus my stay can be
temporary, just a night if you don't mind, and go

ahead and snore. Your heartbeat's white noise
will drift me until dawn's sunlight shards the comforter,

and I unlid, uncurl, unzip, unyawn—spinning, cartoon
bluebirds singing me into the kitchen to start coffee.

When We Watched *The Right Stuff*

Often, when my mind precludes a night's sleep,
I see Sam Shepard galloping alone
in the Mojave, the dusty, orange dusk
bathing him, his chiseled cheeks, an evening
wind parting his thick hair, as he follows
an endless sky, possibility, space.

I think of my basement rental, that space
small, our crisscrossed fingers drifting to sleep
as we watched—so cool how the plane follows
him upside down, breaking mach one, alone.
I'm sure I still see Shepard in evening
skies, flying like Yeager. Do you, too? Dusk

is to blame, how it can confuse and dusk
the memory. Maybe my brain lacks space
to parse the truth so late in the evening,
though ever since that movie, which could sleep
most people in its running time alone,
I feel like my word or thought mis-follows,

each one an earnest rocket that follows
course re-entry yet collides, becomes dusk-
ridden, another piece of junk alone.
If I unlid my eyes now to dark space,
rotate myself to your body in sleep,
will my touch make you know me this evening?

The creamy hand you stroked an evening
summers ago still outlines and follows
your lips oscillating in breath and sleep—
I mean, people say they re-dream, that dusk
lighting in a flashback scene. I feel space,
my fingers' revisits, moments alone—

so come pick a horse, let's set out alone
from our backyard desert, the pink evening
sky our guide to Yeager or Shepard's space.
I am your Barbara Hershey who follows,
each clop a year forward. Forget dusk,
misfired synapses, a need to sleep

alone, your orbit, my body follows.
In space, the evening darkness yields a dusk
every forty minutes, lighting sky's sleep.

Orion's Belt

Today, I am reminded of when
we were the only two left
in the Saturday night quiet,
the dining hall a deserted theme
park where knives and pots
could dance like *Fantasia*, and you
reached for a sandwich
bag's two pills, gulping them
with a kindergartner's-sized carton
of milk. I'm not sure how you
managed to shower, but soon,
we were headed to campus
town, the only time your hand
held mine, skipping me across
the grassy quad, our private
playground. Your eyes glazed
the whole evening—
while we danced to The Dead
cover band and ordered more
pitchers—and you could not
unsmile. You, this memory,
come to me now, as I stare
into a broken-bottled parking
lot, my view from the strip mall's
patio, and I wonder what fated
them there, if like we did all
those weekends ago, drinkers
staired up to the Chemistry
Annex's roof, pretended
to know constellations
while swigging Stroh's Lights,
and you convinced me
to toss ours down, no regard
for any person or chained bike
or bird below, just our shared,
empty hands under the moon.

The More You Know

In between cake pop bites and watching a dinosaur video,
my friend's four-year-old rises from his coffee shop chair.
Don't you know, he asks me, *sharks have no bones*? I tell him
I don't know that, which is true and weird considering how
many years more I am, but what logic he shares knowing
so much about cartilage and connective tissue, and I thank
him, as his long-lashed eyes lower to the phone's screen.

Later, I tell my husband, who smiles over my narration,
about my lesson. He responds—before I can tell him
I know what he will say—"Did you know the human
head weighs eight pounds?", a favorite line from a favorite
film, that six-year-old kid too cute with his factoids
and frontal lisp, and we laugh, my left hand stroking
the baby softness of his neck, as we merge the highway.

That time my face flushed, and the ER doc ordered
blood, we were fine with the possibility, textbook aged
to parent, employed, we could to this, we told each
other, and even these years later, I still feel relief
the results proved negative, I think he would agree—

though had I been more hospitable, I bet we would
know that bees smell fear, *Apatosaurus* the correct name
for Brontosaurus, every day, questions would never
stop, rising one atop the other, hundreds of feet
above the ground, like the tallest trees in the world,
the California Sequoias, we would hear, a small voice
informing from the car's back seat.

Chori

He pulls his father's body out
of his pants pocket, an old film
roll carrier, one among many
he found lining his father's desk
the day a van repossessed the hospital
bed, its size just right to keep
his father near, air-tight enough
not to leak any minerals or decalcify.

The bus he rides into eight hours
of darkness moves to Durango,
cousins his father kicked cans
with after school, a yellow sky.
Un sombrero de vaquero, he says
tapping the container's top,
he can't recall his father with no
hat, even when he no longer left
the house, and they spent hours
watching soccer, shouting *Puto*
along with the stadium fans
to the other team's goalkeeper.

On a last night, the light from
his father's television awoke
the son who didn't mind
moving toward the bright, a tired
body. When he arrived
at the room's door, he thought he
might be in an old photograph,
this man who had to be his father,
sitting upright, eyes wide, unyellowed,
as the *Rockford Files'* theme played
its last, synthesized notes.

Maybe the father felt his son nearby,
since he turned his smile to the door

saying *Mijo* and pointing to the screen,
his son following the finger to Jim
and his father Rocky waxing poetic
about "awful nice ladies" over
the morning percolator. How many
times the son could recall unfolding
tv trays with his own father to watch
Rockford, they would all eat tacos,
Jim's favorite breakfast food, the son
and his father's always *con chorizo*,
his father's childhood nickname. On this

night, the son nodded to his father,
the Rockfords, and walked to the head-
board's rustic post where his father's
cowboy hat rested. Placing it on
his father's head, he asked if he might
like some eggs, perhaps some sausage
while he watched, his father clapping
lightly his son's cheek in response.

His son walked to the kitchen not needing
to turn on any lights, his father's glow
melding into the stove's pilot flame,
the fridge's bulb, the dimmed
streetlamp coloring his father's
house, he cracked and sizzled
in cast iron pans, plating large
mounds for them to share,
so soon they were passing hot
sauce, *pimienta, por favor*, they ate
and laughed in sepia, losing track
of episodes, their neighbors'
cars leaving for industrial parks,
yellow poppies opening for the sun.

My Inability to Remember the Dry Cleaner's Name

I auditioned for Jeopardy once
at a car dealership in Illinois.
We sat in folding chairs,
and I knew Othello had gifted
Desdemona his mother's handkerchief,
and Lago, Nigeria's capital. That was
round one, intimate and informal like
the neighbor's garage bar last Halloween,
where we mingled among Power Rangers
and watched red Solo cups mushroom
our lawns. A week later, I chose
a tweed dress suit and drove
downtown to the same Hilton
lobby Harrison Ford runs through
in The Fugitive, hoping he'd make
an encore cameo.

That day, hundreds filled every chair,
barstool and Travertine step, their heads
down to read almanacs, Shakespeare's Collected
Works, yet I arrived with bottled water
and the Tribune. Before long, we were
all ushered away, again more chairs,
rows and rows yielding a giant screen,
Alex Trebek's large face instructing
us how to respond. I knew Judy Garland
was born Ethel Gumm, Picasso's friendship
with Matisse, but guessed many, Galapagos
Islands for New Zealand, since I liked
its many syllables, its sounds, until
I missed the cut by five, leaving
those who lobby-studied to cheer
and cry their victory, while I exited
the hotel toward Lake Michigan,
the only Great Lake entirely within
the borders of the United States.

There's No Place Like

Homeroom, where the clock hand pendulates
like in that Risky Business scene, moving backwards
before passing the number seven, I watch it
every day, and the smells--apple pectin shampoo
mixed with the football team's ongoing fundraiser,
two glazed Krispy Kremes only twenty five cents--
mask announcements about today's pep
rally and tickets for Saturday's musical. I look up
at the perforated speaker muffling our vice principal's
voice before I turn to the desks, surveying, missing her
teeth
that bit me in preschool and accelerated a second
tetanus booster;
that sang "May We Entertain You" when she was nine—
she came late to school that whole week of Gypsy—
and in every community theater production since;
that now might be clicking Doublemint or chewing
Red Vines, or perhaps chattering, I've heard Kansas
is cold, and I imagine windows open as she drove
her parents' Corolla north, west, her own musical, a girl
from Miami Beach passing cows, purple, not knowing
those fields grew alfalfa, maybe looking for Oz—
she could totally wear her long curls in Dorothy pigtails—
maybe running out of gas or lyrics or truancy, I don't know
why she left, maybe
her teeth
needed to tell how she no longer liked being on stage,
people watching her,
pretending.

Now, the first period bell pivots me, and I crisscross
my bag, so I see that forearm scar, tiny incisor indentations
her Morse code, so many words ago, those teeth so busy,
but I've grown into them, their Orion's Belt configuration

mirroring my asymmetrical ear piercings, and the way
they feel, the depressions, when I grow restless, like now,
as I pass her empty seat.

The Dental Office

Today's feature in *The Stafford Courier* is about the culvert
repair on Highway 281, just outside of Seward. I know this

because the two men in the waiting room, one wearing a seed
hat and overalls, the other in a western shirt and jeans, read

sections aloud. Every so often I smile over at them, we are
sharing this time together, after all, and I imagine their lives,

routines, thinking they might enjoy being indoors this June
Wednesday instead of out in the field. I want to comment

on today's wind or ask if they had much rain with last night's
storm—this is Kansas, where weather promises constant

conversation—yet I hesitate, presume that this, despite
the backgrounding Christian rock and muffled, drill noises

from the back, might be the quiet and calm of their day, no hot
wind whipping the shelterbelt junipers, no alfalfa baler yawps,

no voices yelling about irrigation levels across the shaggy, hay
rows. Even when the tornado sirens sound at noon, no one

speaks or moves, this being the first of the month at noon
and test day, so I return to my novel, listen for when their friend

thanks the assistant for her fresh toothbrush and mini paste, only
too pleased when, when on their way out, the overalled man, taps

my left shoulder, says, "It's all up to you now," and we laugh, my eyes
following through the office window, as they exit in haloed sunlight.

Part III:

Outer Space

Ten Suggestions for How to Be a Good Boyfriend

I.
Make plans to meet for dinner, but don't
arrive early, order before she has arrived,
and finish eating. When she eats her big
salad alone, your "I was hungry" won't
make her feel any less awkward, in spite
of how you smile at the dangling alfalfa
sprouting from her lips.

II.
Do encourage your girlfriend to go home,
drink juice, crawl into bed, and disconnect
the phone when her head explodes
with snot, just don't forget your advice,
then run across campus town (when you
are not in shape to run) to her house, fling
open her bedroom door and scream, "Why
haven't you been answering the phone?"

III.
Remember her birthday on her birthday.
Yes, a Michelle Shocked cd and sweater
make lovely gifts six days later, and she
doesn't want generic, heart-shaped jewelry
from the mall, but you should lodge her,
like a looping song, in your brain,
in your memory, in you.

IV.
Don't lean over at the R.E.M. concert
to mutter, "I think I left the French fryer
on," then go back to singing along
with the band. She, having survived
a house fire, will tug your shirt the rest

of the show, will want to check the house,
will miss the band performing her favorite
song right in front of her.

V.
Don't sleep with another woman, especially
if she has the same name. Sure, there's
the convenience of only one name to moan
during sex, but she watches the other
woman brush her tits against you, when
you're at the bar, finds her little
notes left on the kitchen counter—
that's another issue, for God's sake: hide
what your girlfriend need not see—
and knows the tenor of your "nothing
happened" denials, your voice sounding
modified, like in those *60 Minutes* segments.

VI.
Always say, "Good night, sweet baby,"
as you kiss her before bed.

VII.
Wash dishes while playing harmonica.
The holder always makes her laugh, plus
you are really good. Likewise, when you
become a math teacher in a few years
and she picks you up at the junior high,
strum guitar for the lone student needing
after school help, then play his request
of the *Gilligan's Island* theme after
he's understood fractions, all while
she watches, enframed by the classroom
door.

VIII.
Slide the glass doors, so the stray kitty
can enter from the parking lot, then open
a can of tuna, serve, and continue watching
the Machu Picchu documentary while the kitty
eats, thanks you, says he'll see you tomorrow.
She will hug you long after that.

IX.
Don't die in a motorcycle accident. Two days
before your birthday, four days before you
will be together for Christmas. You and she
will be at the end of the long-distance years,
ready to move forward, buy a house, be
in the same state. Just don't.

X.
When you're gone, send her someone, someone you
would play pool and have beers with, someone who
laughs at her jokes, someone who listens to her stories
of you, someone who loves her family and builds a structure
for the outside strays, someone who calms her, rubs her ear,
surprises her with favorite beer, writes her messages on the
kitchen
whiteboard, dances when she finds her *Saturday Night Fever*
album, someone who stays.

Four on the Floor

You tell me you like house music—
how the synthesized thumps traverse your veins,
hippocampus, so you are twenty again,
the exotic American, dancing
with strangers and pint glasses
at Le Beat Route.

Then there is the music of house—
the fridge's decade-old respirations;
unsettled, foundation cracks;
the a/c's throbbings, constant, desperate, unsyncopated;
they make me think of Jodie Foster lying
in a New Mexican array, that movie scene
where concussive transmissions arouse her
to finger her headphones,
to reaffirm space.

I think about space, too,
all kinds: nebulas; mileage;
caesuras; naked fingers; the gap
my night brace never fixed; how you space
yourself when you tell a story, your space
so close our shoulders fuse,
as you shift from heel to heel,
trying to meet my steady beat—

until you back into
the blocks, the no loitering signs
between our houses,
leaving me to listen
to your absence and
the spaces between my breaths.

Orbital Debris

Two guys manhug
on the other side of the gas pump.
They catch each other
up on jobs, family, until I hear one say,
"Nothing to lose sleep over,"
and I lose myself in the cliché,
so much so that I don't feel
how the clicks,
in my gripped handle,
have stopped.

I do lose
sleep, night after night,
clumps that must orbit
the universe
like abandoned satellites, clamp bands,
or separation bolts from past missions.
I can't forget the earthquake
victims, my coworker's diagnosis.
Beneath my lids, I see
a former lover's back,
a dead cat in the shower,
while the hours elude and entice
my gravitational pull.

On His Way to See a Man

For Maria Luisa

Over coffee, my friend tells me how he drove to Juarez
with his mother's dresses, his father wanting only one
as a remembrance. When he'd piled them into the truck bed,
he found himself zippering a sleeveless, checkered, jumper,
a clichéd movie gesture he couldn't stop
right away.

His father told him where to go, to a man who knew
his mother, his family, their pre-American life, a man
who could offer *condolencias* when my friend arrived
at his door, outstretching his arm *a la sala de estar*,
wooden rosaries adorning the walls and closets
holding others' suits and skirts for later
redressing.

So, he traveled south, listening to the plastic hangers'
rattle, their syncing with the tires' rotations, circle into circle,
click after click, like a coded message, his mother's calm
jarring him to attention.

When driving onto Eje Vial Juan Gabriel, only miles
from the man's house, my friend turned
pink, the sunset's streaks warming his windshield,
his face, all around him, a city bathed, the aura
so strong it divined the car past the man's street,
trajecting ahead until my friend arrived
at one of the pink cross clusters
commemorating so many murders,
young women not to be forgotten. Once there,
still blushing in the late day's light, he exited
the truck for the matching crosses, and one
by one, draped them in his mother.

The Space Between

For years, I've dreamt about losing my teeth.
Sometimes they all fall out, disintegrate,
like skeeted pigeons,
while other times, one
by one, they dribble out of my mouth.

The dreams remind me of when I was six,
and my parents' friends invited us to dinner,
their house an indoor playground: orange, shag
lawns; polka-dotted, mushroom candles;
hanging beads as doorways.
We ate barbequed ribs so big,
my dad called them "Brontosaurus-sized"
and made jokes about Fred and Wilma.

I am meeting friends for dinner in a foreign city.
The cab yields to my practiced hand, so I settle
in, anonymous, adventurous,
alone. We glide along a rainy street—
where porches compete and shiny sedans
abut abandoned gloves—
until the driver stops:
Do I go left or right here? Which way? Which way?
I laugh, then ask if I'm being punked,
but he neither smiles nor turns to me,
only jerks his head from left to right.
At that moment, I remember
that no one knows—

I'm with this man, in this cab that lingers
at a darkened intersection, a polite gesture
no other drivers behold.
I see no dogs, no neon,
just shards of water disappearing

into the Potomac's veneer.

My favorite part was the hickory sauce,
and when I asked for more,
my dad told me to smile.
For almost two weeks, I had wiggled
my tongue against the two, lose ones
on the bottom, yet now they were gone—
digested with corn, gristle, red strands
of cabbage—detained
in the duodenum.
The loss so sudden, I felt cheated—no
proper goodbye nor placement under my pillow—
and scared, but my dad assured me they'd not stay
with me forever—that I'd be fine—
and soon, my tongue flipped around
the newly-vacated space.

In The First Row of the National Cathedral

A week after his departure, she sits on the aisle,
so everyone who eulogizes can reach her hand
after descending the marble steps, nod in sync
with her pillboxed head, as the choir sings
"The Battle Hymn's" second verse.

No matter how many times she bows her chin,
turns to cheek a well-wisher's lips, tears up
during a reading from Corinthians, that hat—
black, inlayed, its gentle leaves beginning to vine
down her neck—does not budge, so stubborn
the securing pins are to her scalp, her stoicism.
She doesn't even recall dressing for today, who
suggested the hat, its asymmetry and distraction.

Still, how fitting it would be, she thinks, if he could
unfasten it now, a Chantilly Frisbee he could pilot
toward the tabernacle, spontaneous, charming,
so soon, from the pews all would rise in a long-armed
wave like at the baseball game, his laughs escaping
from the mahogany casket and bouncing along
the grand chamber.

Hours from now, when relatives have turned on
the college game and encouraged her to eat
a room-service sandwich, she will excuse herself
to draw a bath, disrobe, the week a black mound
in the room's corner, and she will try to break free,
fingering the hat pins, her head—shaking back,
left, up, again—trying, too, all while she lowers
into the filling water, wishing her fingers
teeth—

his teeth that bit open the Mae West jacket

after his Skyhawk was shot down, his arms
and leg too fractured to assist, those teeth

        preserving his life and rising him to the water's
        surface,

those teeth that could rip the hat in one motion,
        smile at her relief, mouth her name one last
        time, those teeth

her pruning fingers float out of the water for, past
        the void on her head, and into his air.

Time Out

No one forgets the crunch, the gooeyness left
on the Spanish tile or in the air, the collision
when nightly stroll meets a flip flop's bottom,
deconstructed circle, smeared, snail's entrails
scooped into a paper towel. This is a hazard
living humid, where children's fingers, like rockets
shedding fiery parts, capture lizard tails that keep
moving long after torsos scurry, and roaches
cuddle in dishwasher dispensers until the heating
element whirls, and detergent intoxicates. No matter
how many gnats seep through the screening holes
or refilled water dishes line the yard, there is no
denying this legacy, its evolutionary seeping
into protoplasm, inertia as heavy as days soaked
in skunk and overripe citrus, souring stomachs,
the air, any chance to move away.

Had We Known Our Time

I didn't know then how fixed our time—
only four months until you'd lay
under an overpass, the dented
helmet still on your head, some stranger
holding your heavy hand.
If I did, we would have kept driving,
recorded your voice,
thrown my diaphragm in the dumpster.

We'd have driven a cooler car,
your father's beige Chrysler too geriatric
for runs to the drive-through liquor marts.
Away from bell schedules, pressed
clothes and parents, we'd head east
into a series of clichés: a toothless mechanic,
his corroded pickup home to chains,
crushed cans, a three-legged dog named Ringo;
the Sangre sky of a moist, July afternoon;
and rabbits as huge as the jackalopes
jumping off the billboards near casinos.

We could have visited the Atomic Museum,
where you'd wear a tie-dye. At Coronado Monument,
we'd stroll the maze of open-roof dwellings
while you'd serenade—guitar strapped
against your chest, the harmonica
at your chin looking like a neck brace.
You'd play my requests, "Lay Down Sally,"
"Meet Me in the Morning,"
until you'd wander away, leave me the lone tourist
circling the ruin of our lives.

Acknowledgements

"Chori," *Euphony*
"Four on the Floor," *Vallum: Contemporary Poetry*
"Had We Known Our Time,"   *Prime Number Magazine*
"Incubation," *Eunoia Review*
"In The First Row of the National Cathedral," *Heartwood*
"Living Below Sea Level," *Rattle*
"Mimeograph," *Broad River Review*
"My Inability to Remember the Drycleaner's Name," *Smartish
        Pace*
"No Shoes Required," *Red Eft Review*
"On His Way to See a Man," *Solstice: A Magazine of Diverse
        Voices* (Editors' Pick)
"Orion's Belt," *Snapdragon*
"Ten Suggestions for How to Be a Good Boyfriend,"
        Common Ground Review
"The Dental Office," *Clementine Unbound*
"The More You Know," *Slippery Elm*
"The Space Between," *Scapegoat Review* (forthcoming 2022)
"Time Out," *Euphony*
"Why Is It?," *Garbanzo Literary Journal*
"When We Watched *The Right Stuff*," *Radar Poetry*
"You, Yourself, Are Still Okay," *Box of Matches*
"You Always Knew," *Garbanzo Literary Journal*

Laura Read's Comments for selecting this chapbook:

I admire the way this collection is organized in three sections:
Ground Control, Breathing Space, and Outer Space, and how
the space motif, emphasized by the opening epigraph from Carl
Sagan, provides unity for this collection. This unity is also
created through the repetition and alternation of various
themes, including memories of childhood, snapshots of a
marriage, and elegies for friends lost, children not had, time
going by. Each poem is well-crafted with attention to imagery,
so I felt like I was a part of the speaker's world; for example, in
one of my favorite poems in the collection, "Living Below Sea
Level," the speaker describes their longing for hurricanes for
"that chance/ to masking tape our windows in 'Xs'," which is
such an exact image that captures a child's mind and the
experience of living in a particular place. I also love the poem's
ending: "So often, though, no winds/ ruptured palm fronds, no
storm eye quieted, no school/ got cancelled, in spite of our
loyalty, our sacrifice,/ our willingness to monitor, that taping
and alarm naught,/ our only celebration some early morning
chocolate milk/ and extra bowls of Alpha Bits." These lines
capture something I really like in this book: each poem is a
small moment that contains something bigger when observed
and described closely, a small piece of orbital debris.

Laura Read is the author of *Dresses from the Old Country*,
Instructions for My Mother's Funeral, and *The Chewbacca on Hollywood
Boulevard Reminds Me of You*. She won the 2012 AWP Donald
Hall Prize for Poetry and the 2011 Floating Bridge Press
Chapbook Award.

About the Author:

Amy Lerman was born and raised on Miami Beach, moved to the Midwest for many years, and now lives with her husband and very spoiled cats in the Arizona desert, so all three landscapes figure prominently into her writing. She is residential English Faculty at Mesa Community College, and her poems have appeared in or are forthcoming in *Willawaw Journal*, *Stonecoast Review*, *Broad River Review*, *Radar Poetry*, *Rattle*, *Slippery Elm*, and other publications. Her poem, "Why Is It?" was the inaugural winner of the Art Young Memorial Award for Poetry.

The **Jonathan Holden Poetry Chapbook Contest** is an annual competition for poets who have not yet published a chapbook or full-length collection of poems.

Choeofpleirn Press accepts manuscripts for the contest between January 1 and the last Sunday of April every year.

Submissions should be 25-40 pages of poetry organized by the poet and saved as one file. The collection may include poems published individually in literary magazines or elsewhere. All submissions are considered for publication, but only the winner receives $250 and 10 copies of the print version of the chapbook.

All poets who submit to the contest and pay the $20 contest fee will receive an ebook copy of the winning chapbook (a $15 value).

See our website for submission details: www.choeofpleirnpress.com.

The **Kenneth Johnston Nonfiction Book Award** is an annual creative nonfiction book contest that runs from the first week of September through the end of December.

See our website for submission details: www.choeofpleirnpress.com.

Choeofpleirn Press publishes four annual literary magazines. *Coneflower Café* is devoted to fiction, poetry, and art. *Glacial Hills Review* focuses on nonfiction, poetry, and art. *Rushing Thru the Dark* features one-act plays and short screenplays, poetry, and art. The *Best of Choeofopleirn Press* issue showcases the best selections from our five annual creative contests in fiction, nonfiction, drama, poetry, and art.

See our website for submission details: www.choeofpleirnpress.com.

Fun fact:

Choeofpleirn is pronounced "chuf-plern," and is a combination of the two founders' surnames, but roughly means "chief place of rest."

Choeofpleirn Press
www.choeofpleirnpress.com
choeofpleirnpress@gmail.com